Mayflower
1620

Christian Jr./Sr. High School
2100 Greenfield Dr
El Cajon, CA 92019

Mayflower 1620

A NEW LOOK AT
A PILGRIM VOYAGE

PLIMOTH PLANTATION

WITH PETER ARENSTAM, JOHN KEMP,
and CATHERINE O'NEILL GRACE

Photographs by SISSE BRIMBERG
and COTTON COULSON

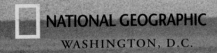
NATIONAL GEOGRAPHIC
WASHINGTON, D.C.

Table of Contents

Foreword

NANCY BRENNAN, EXECUTIVE DIRECTOR, PLIMOTH PLANTATION

IN THE HARBOR OF Plymouth, Massachusetts, an old-fashioned wooden ship called *Mayflower II* floats beside a pier near Plymouth Rock. Every year, many thousands of people come aboard. They want to learn about the original *Mayflower* and the founding of Plymouth Colony back in 1620.

Plimoth Plantation, a living history museum, has exhibited *Mayflower II* since 1957. Maritime artisans and other dedicated professionals work to keep the ship in her best sailing condition. In the past ten years, they have had her out to sea under sail several times.

Staff members appreciate *Mayflower II* as a unique "time machine" that enables them to get the feel of sea travel in colonial days. To understand more about ship design, construction, and the skills needed to sail in the 17th century, they study ongoing research in marine archaeology, colonial boat-building, and woodworking.

Just as important is understanding more about the seamen who sailed *Mayflower* and the passengers who traveled on it for 66 days on their way to an unfamiliar country. This book offers new images both of the ship and of the many different people who are part of its story, including the Native people who inhabited North America long before Europeans arrived.

On the reproduction ship Mayflower II, *trained role players called interpreters portray the 17th-century people who sailed on the original* Mayflower.

ABOARD *MAYFLOWER*

*I*t was dark, rainy, and cold out on the open Atlantic, and the ship pitched and rolled. There were no other vessels on the tossing waves. The travelers on *Mayflower* were alone. It was autumn 1620. The ship's passengers—102 in all—did not think they were sailing into history. They were more concerned about the weather. But this wind-tossed ship they traveled in would become an important symbol in the history of the United States.

History is complicated. People sailed on *Mayflower* for different reasons. The passengers hoped to start new lives in America. The sailors just had a job to do. Across the Atlantic, the native Wampanoag did not expect this ship, which would ultimately lead to the loss of their land and way of life.

There are only two firsthand accounts of *Mayflower*'s voyage. William Bradford wrote a few pages on the crossing in his history, *Of Plymouth Plantation*. *Mourt's Relation*, another contemporary account of Plymouth Colony's beginnings, gives even less information about the journey.

For this book we sailed the reproduction ship *Mayflower II* to bring to life the experience of the people who crossed the Atlantic in 1620. The ship itself is about 100 feet long and has three masts, six sails, and miles of rope rigging. Aboard her, we can begin to understand what it must have been like to spend two months at sea on a small merchant vessel. Aboard her, we can better understand our history. Sailing her is a rare opportunity. Come along.

A crew of 26 helped sail Mayflower II *on Cape Cod Bay for this book.*
As on the original Mayflower, *sailors kept lookout from atop the sail at the front of the ship, known as the spritsail.*

SEEKING "NEW WORLDS"

"Such as in ships and brittle barkes unto the seas descend."

PSALM 107, V. 23, STERNHOLD & HOPKINS PSALTER, 1618 EDITION

When *Mayflower* sailed in 1620, Europe was in turmoil. Religious differences fueled hostilities between Protestant nations, such as England and Holland, and Catholic nations, such as France and Spain. These four countries were competing with each other to establish colonies across the Atlantic. The timber, fish, furs, and other abundant natural resources found there could be harvested by colonists and sent back to Europe to increase the mother country's wealth and power. The Europeans gave little thought to the rights of the Native people already living in the Americas.

Mayflower's passengers and crew were not the first Europeans to travel to the northeast coast of North America. Fishing vessels had been sailing to the area since the early 1500s to take advantage of its rich fishing grounds. And before 1620, at least six explorers had visited the region that the Wampanoag—

Mayflower's rigging was made of miles of hemp cordage, or ropes. Each line had a purpose. Standing rigging secured the masts and yards in place. Running rigging moved through wooden blocks to control the sails.

More than 100 passengers with their belongings, including some small farm animals and a small workboat, competed for space with Mayflower's sailors, officers, and the ship's supplies. During the stormy crossing, the passengers spent most of their time belowdecks (1). When not working the ship, the sailors could find a hot meal in the cook room located in the forecastle (2). Spare equipment and supplies were stored in the hold (3). From the poop deck, above the roundhouse, Master Christopher Jones could see out to the horizon and view all the workings of the ship (4). Officers working on the half deck (5) relayed commands to the helmsman in the steerage cabin (6). Sailors hoisted heavy sails with the aid of a rotating cylinder known as the capstan (7) and raised the anchor with the hauling device called a windlass (8).

the Native people living there—called Patuxet. One of these was Captain John Smith, an Englishman who helped settle Jamestown, Virginia. Smith's 1614 map of the area was the first to use the names *Plymouth* and *New England*.

The English looked to the New World for a natural resource that was running out on their own island. They needed lumber, and lots of it! To fight wars and establish colonies, the English had been busy building warships and merchant vessels—all from lumber. Over the years, the shipbuilding boom had used up much of England's forests. Forges burned yet more wood to make ironwork for ships and guns. In the year 1610, more than 140 forges in one part of England consumed 80,000 trees. To the English, America's woodlands offered a seemingly endless supply of timber. *Mayflower's* passengers hoped such valuable resources would make their colony profitable.

To get to North America, passengers and crew needed vessels large and sturdy enough to carry all the supplies necessary for the long voyage. Decks had to be strong enough to support large guns, which were needed for protection against pirates and other enemies. The ships also had to stand up to the strain of sailing for months on the open sea. *Mayflower* was one of these seaworthy vessels.

Mayflower *carried many kinds of equipment. The colonists brought tools they would need in the New World, such as nets and traps for fishing. The sailors needed navigational equipment, such as the spool of line with an attached lead weight. This device was used to measure the depth of the ocean.*

DEPARTURE

"They put to sea...with a prosperous wind."

WILLIAM BRADFORD, *Of Plymouth Plantation*

Early in the summer of 1620, a young boy named Francis Billington stood with the crowd on one of the many docks lining London's River Thames. A fleet of vessels, large and small, came and went along the busy river. Some were headed for English ports, others for European destinations, their holds filled with trade goods. Still others were military ships full of sailors, soldiers, and guns. Of all these ships, very few had ever sailed across the Atlantic. But Francis and his family were going to America. They would be among the passengers boarding the merchant ship *Mayflower.*

Once on the ship, the Billingtons must have gone belowdecks to survey the small space allotted to them. Along with 70 or 80 other passengers, they had to work out their own accommodations in the orlop, a large open under-deck meant for carrying freight. Some built small cabins, no bigger than a large

---

A ship of 180 tons fills up quickly! The colonists needed tools, armaments, and even some livestock, along with enough food and drink to last them until their first harvest. The crew needed enough provisions for the journey back home as well.

Eager to depart, passengers had to endure a month of delays before finally leaving from Plymouth, England.

bed, while others simply placed straw-filled mattresses on the deck.

Before setting out to sea, *Mayflower*'s master, Christopher Jones, had his crew work the vessel along the south coast of England to Southampton. There they took on more supplies and passengers and met up with a smaller ship, *Speedwell,* which was coming from Holland to join them in sailing to America.

In early August 1620, *Mayflower* and *Speedwell* put to sea. The officers shouted out orders from the half deck. The mariners swarmed in the rigging. The mates ordered young sailors, not much older than Francis, up the masts to set the topsails. Older mariners prepared to haul up the anchor. When all was ready, Master Jones called out to set sail. As *Mayflower* surged through the water, the sound of the bow wave curling away from the hull echoed between the decks.

The passengers had little time to adjust to the motion of the sea before Master Reynolds of *Speedwell* signaled trouble. His ship was taking on water. It had to return to harbor twice, first at Dartmouth, then at Plymouth. The colonists finally decided not to risk an ocean crossing in such an untrustworthy vessel. They would make do with just *Mayflower.*

While provisions were transferred from *Speedwell,* difficult choices had to be made: How many passengers could

squeeze onto *Mayflower*, and who would they be? Some whole families decided to return home. In other cases, a father came alone, or perhaps with a son, leaving the rest of the family behind. The Billingtons stayed aboard as a family. William Bradford, a *Mayflower* passenger who would become governor of the new colony across the ocean, wrote that some of "the least useful and most unfit" people were persuaded to give up their places to stronger passengers. With 102 passengers and a full crew of sailors crowded aboard, *Mayflower* was ready to depart at last.

Sailors looked forward to a six-month voyage to the New World and back. Mate Clark and Mate Coppin had both been to America on previous passages.

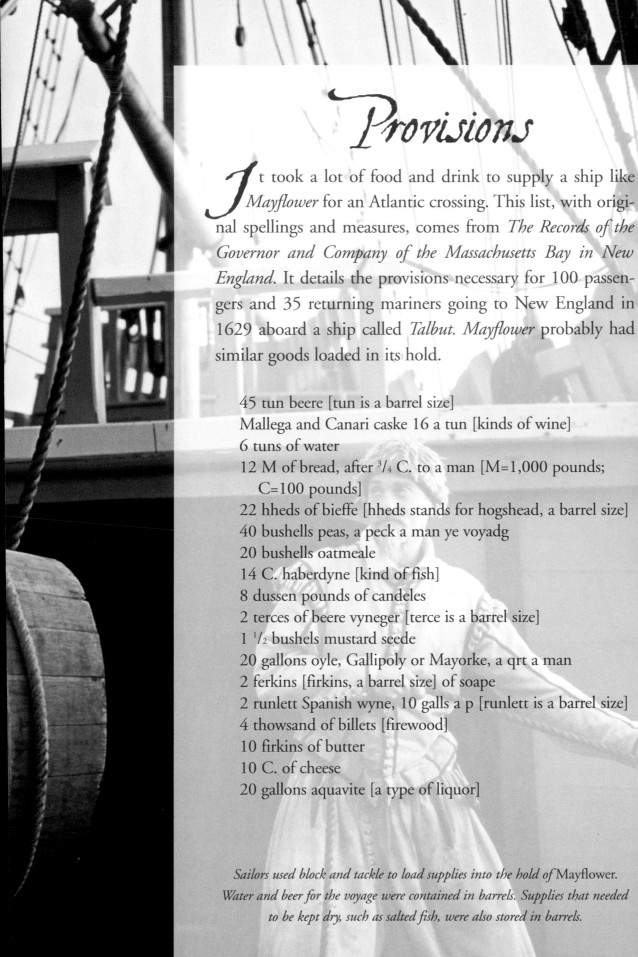

Provisions

*I*t took a lot of food and drink to supply a ship like *Mayflower* for an Atlantic crossing. This list, with original spellings and measures, comes from *The Records of the Governor and Company of the Massachusetts Bay in New England*. It details the provisions necessary for 100 passengers and 35 returning mariners going to New England in 1629 aboard a ship called *Talbut*. *Mayflower* probably had similar goods loaded in its hold.

45 tun beere [tun is a barrel size]
Mallega and Canari caske 16 a tun [kinds of wine]
6 tuns of water
12 M of bread, after $^3/_4$ C. to a man [M=1,000 pounds; C=100 pounds]
22 hheds of bieffe [hheds stands for hogshead, a barrel size]
40 bushells peas, a peck a man ye voyadg
20 bushells oatmeale
14 C. haberdyne [kind of fish]
8 dussen pounds of candeles
2 terces of beere vyneger [terce is a barrel size]
1 $^1/_2$ bushels mustard seede
20 gallons oyle, Gallipoly or Mayorke, a qrt a man
2 ferkins [firkins, a barrel size] of soape
2 runlett Spanish wyne, 10 galls a p [runlett is a barrel size]
4 thowsand of billets [firewood]
10 firkins of butter
10 C. of cheese
20 gallons aquavite [a type of liquor]

Sailors used block and tackle to load supplies into the hold of Mayflower. *Water and beer for the voyage were contained in barrels. Supplies that needed to be kept dry, such as salted fish, were also stored in barrels.*

A VARIED COMPANY

"Readier to go to dispute than to set forward a voyage."

COLONIST ROBERT CUSHMAN, LETTER OF JUNE 10, 1620, WRITTEN WHILE PURCHASING PROVISIONS

Popular myth describes the passengers aboard *Mayflower* as a band of brave Pilgrims setting sail to gain religious freedom in the New World. In reality, they were not a unified group, and they never called themselves Pilgrims. That name was applied two centuries later by historians who took it from William Bradford's *Of Plymouth Plantation*. In a brief passage, Bradford had identified members of his church as pilgrims in a religious sense—that is, they were on a journey seeking God. He never meant his biblical reference to include everyone on board.

Bradford was a leader of a congregation of British Protestants, sometimes called Puritans or Separatists, who had broken away from the national Church of England. Persecuted for their way of worship, they had fled England in 1609 for Holland. After living in exile in the city of Leiden for more than ten years, some

---

Aboard Mayflower *to do a job, not found a colony, the sailors sometimes troubled the passengers with insults and frightening tales. Children had to endure long hours in close quarters during bad weather.*

21

of the church members decided to sail to America to found a colony.

To finance the voyage, the Leiden church members made a deal with a group of English investors known as merchant adventurers. The merchants agreed to pay for the ship and supplies, and the colonists signed a contract promising to work in North America to pay them back. From the start the colonists argued with the investors

In fair weather, passengers were invited to exercise on deck and enjoy fresh air and sunlight. Belowdecks, familiar tasks such as knitting, as well as games and stories, helped to pass the time.

about how much to spend on provisions and about the terms of their contract.

Everyone aboard *Mayflower* hoped to own land and provide a good future for their children. More than half the families had some connection with the Leiden church, and several others may well have agreed with them about the need for religious reform. At least a few, however, were suspicious of Puritans and hostile to the colony's leaders. These differences led to tensions. William Bradford complained about "untoward [difficult and unruly] persons," and identified the Billington family as "one of the profanest [most disrespectful of religion]." He wondered how the Billingtons had been "shuffled into their company."

The colonists differed in other ways as well. They disagreed about who should be allowed to own land and how to organize the group for work once they arrived in the New World. Shopkeepers and tradesmen came from cities and towns, while farmers came from the countryside. The colonists came from many regions and spoke an assortment of dialects. Like their countrymen in England, some knew how to read, while others didn't. None were lords. Some families brought servants; most did not. The colonists did not regard themselves as a group of equals. They reflected the variety found in the middle and lower classes of 17th-century English society.

COLONISTS FROM LEIDEN

18 married couples, 15 with children; 6 married men traveling without their wives, 4 with sons; 8 servants

Five Leading Men

John Carver. Elected first governor of Plymouth Colony but died in the spring of 1621.

William Brewster. Preacher, or "Ruling Elder," from the Leiden church and only university man in the early colony. Former courtier and printer. Persecuted in England for encouraging illegal worship.

William Bradford. Elected second governor of Plymouth Colony. Wrote famous history, *Of Plymouth Plantation.*

Samuel Fuller. Deacon and surgeon.

Edward Winslow. Probably the colonist of highest social rank. Later became assistant governor then governor of Plymouth Colony. He was also sent to England several times as the colony's agent.

COLONISTS FROM ENGLAND

7 married couples, 6 with children; 1 married man traveling without his wife; 5 servants

Five Leading Men

Christopher Martin. Associated with the investors who put up the money for the voyage. Elected governor of the *Mayflower* passengers.

Myles Standish. An English soldier from Lancashire, he evidently became acquainted with the Leiden church (of which he was not a member) while in that city. He commanded the colonial militia.

Stephen Hopkins. He had been in Virginia, so was the only *Mayflower* passenger who had previously crossed the Atlantic. The colonists relied on him in their early dealings with the Wampanoag.

Richard Warren. He left his wife and five daughters home in London. (They arrived in 1623.) He seems to have been one of the stronger supporters of Governor Bradford and the Leiden church.

John Billington. The first man punished before *Mayflower* headed home (for disobeying Captain Standish). William Bradford regarded him as a troublemaker. In 1630, Billington became the first colonist executed for murder.

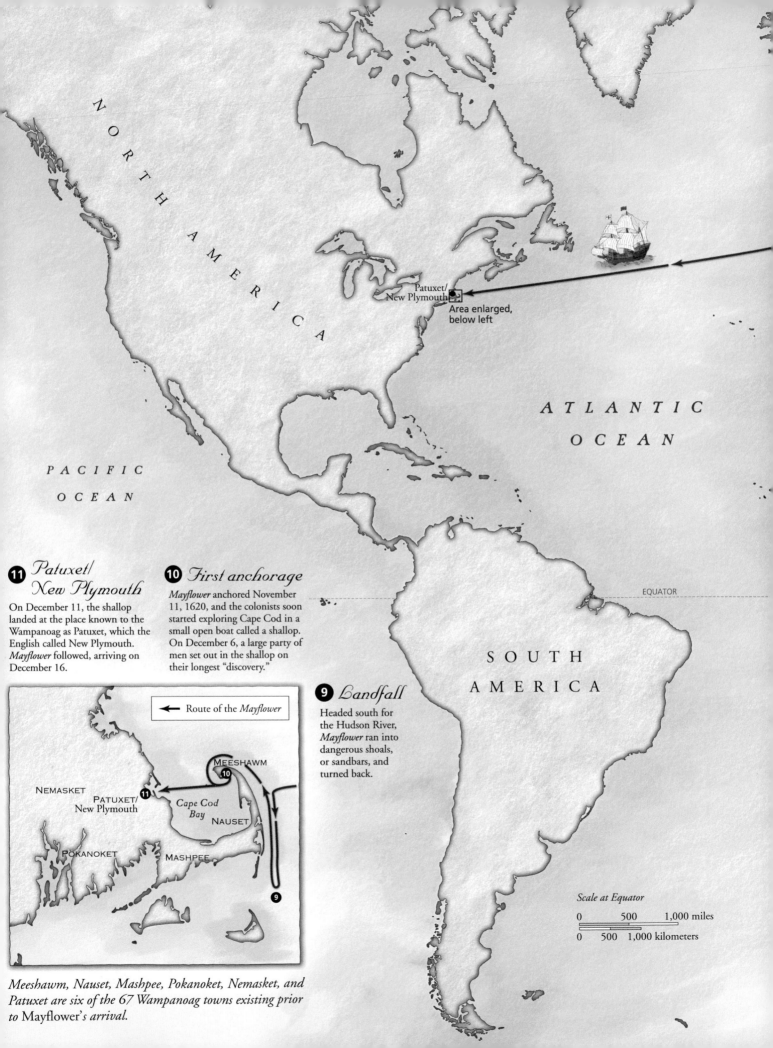

N O R T H   A M E R I C A

PACIFIC
OCEAN

ATLANTIC
OCEAN

Patuxet/
New Plymouth

Area enlarged,
below left

EQUATOR

SOUTH
AMERICA

**⑪ Patuxet/
New Plymouth**

On December 11, the shallop
landed at the place known to the
Wampanoag as Patuxet, which the
English called New Plymouth.
Mayflower followed, arriving on
December 16.

⑩ First anchorage

Mayflower anchored November
11, 1620, and the colonists soon
started exploring Cape Cod in a
small open boat called a shallop.
On December 6, a large party of
men set out in the shallop on
their longest "discovery."

⑨ Landfall

Headed south for
the Hudson River,
Mayflower ran into
dangerous shoals,
or sandbars, and
turned back.

⟵ Route of the *Mayflower*

MEESHAWM

NEMASKET

PATUXET/
New Plymouth

⑪

Cape Cod
Bay

NAUSET

POKANOKET

MASHPEE

⑩

⑨

Scale at Equator

| 0 | 500 | 1,000 miles |

| 0 | 500 | 1,000 kilometers |

*Meeshawm, Nauset, Mashpee, Pokanoket, Nemasket, and
Patuxet are six of the 67 Wampanoag towns existing prior
to* Mayflower's *arrival.*

Mayflower's Journey

EUROPE

Great Britain

Plymouth

Area enlarged, below right

ASIA

AFRICA

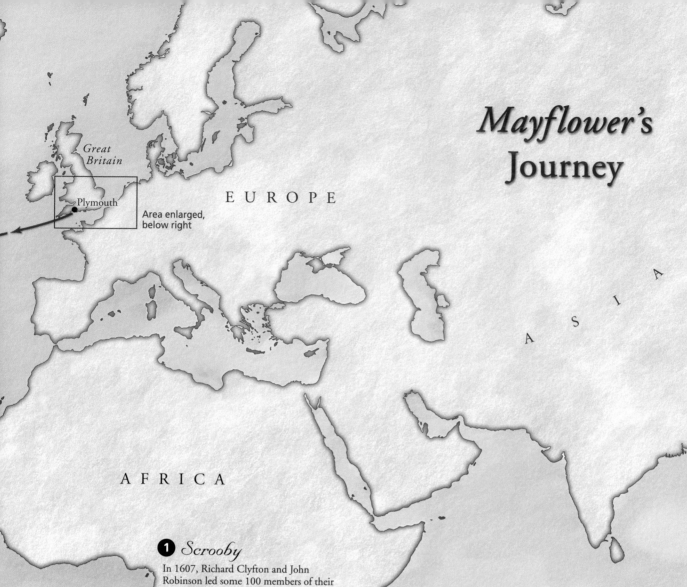

1 Scrooby

In 1607, Richard Clyfton and John Robinson led some 100 members of their outlawed religious congregation from Scrooby into exile in Amsterdam. Holland was well known as a country that tolerated different religions. Among the congregation were future colonial leaders John Carver, William Brewster, and William Bradford.

2 Amsterdam

In 1609–1610, after disputes with other exiled English churches in Amsterdam, John Robinson led a congregation that settled in Leiden, another town in Holland.

3 Leiden

By 1616, members of the Leiden church were unhappy with life in Holland and began to think about moving to America. After a few unsuccessful proposals, they began talks with Englishman Thomas Weston about founding a new colony.

4 London

In the spring of 1620, Thomas Weston and about 70 other investors put up money to begin a colony in North America. At least 50 people from England were ready to join members of the Leiden church in the venture.

5 Delftshaven

Early in the summer of 1620, members of the Leiden church purchased a small ship, *Speedwell*, "of some 60 tun," compared to *Mayflower*'s 180. They boarded in this Dutch port and sailed to Southampton in England to meet *Mayflower*. They hoped to sail the two ships together across the Atlantic.

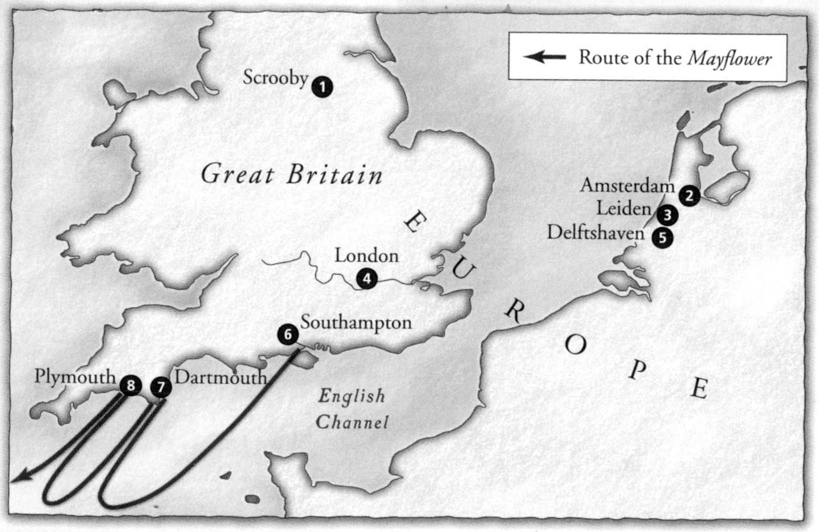

8 Plymouth

After further troubles with *Speedwell*, the colonists decided to leave that ship behind. They chose from among them 102 passengers, who crowded aboard *Mayflower* and finally departed on September 6, 1620.

Inset map labels

Scrooby 1

⬅ Route of the *Mayflower*

Great Britain

Amsterdam 2
Leiden 3
Delftshaven 5

London 4

Southampton 6

EUROPE

Plymouth 8 7 Dartmouth

English Channel

7 Dartmouth

With *Speedwell* leaking, the two ships put in at Dartmouth for repairs, setting out again a few weeks later.

6 Southampton

In late July, *Mayflower* and *Speedwell* took on final supplies and passengers. Despite disagreements about money, supplies, and their contract, the colonists at last departed on August 5, 1620.

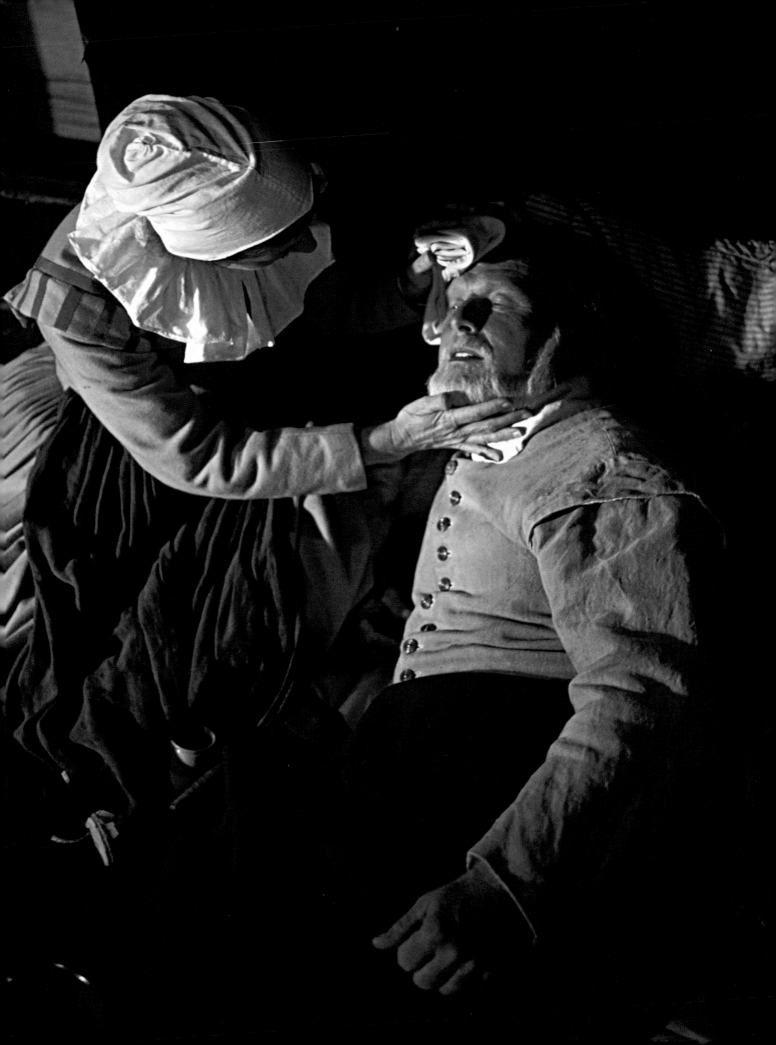

THE VOYAGE

"...the vast ocean, and a sea of troubles...."

WILLIAM BRADFORD, *OF PLYMOUTH PLANTATION*

On September 6, 1620, *Mayflower* left the dock at Plymouth, England, and set out alone for the New World. All the passengers had experienced at least two other ship departures by then and must have begun to see familiar patterns. What appeared to be chaos among men and rigging slowly evolved into the smooth operation of a ship under sail. The passengers must have felt encouraged by the week of fair weather they had at the start of their voyage. Some of them could handle the constant motion of the ship, whereas others, even in calm weather, were seasick.

Soon autumn gales began to blow. As William Bradford told it, "They were encountered many times with crosswinds and met with fierce storms, with which the ship was shroudly [viciously] shaken, and her upper works made very leaky." Several accounts tell of ships in the 17th century that suffered damage in storms.

Few of Mayflower's *passengers had been to sea before. Weeks of rough weather and wet conditions belowdecks made many people sick. Some passengers stayed weak and ill even after the ship arrived in America.*

Passenger John Howland had to be helped back aboard after being pitched into the sea by the wildly tossing Mayflower.

Some vessels lost their masts and rigging to the sea. One ill-fated ship lost its entire forward cabin, including the cook room and all the people working there. By comparison, *Mayflower* was lucky. During her stormy passage she suffered only a bowed and cracked main deck beam. While this frightened some mariners and passengers enough to suggest turning back to England, the ship's carpenter quickly had the damaged beam repaired.

Still, the danger to the passengers and crew remained. Bradford relates that "in sundry of these storms the winds were so fierce and the seas so high, as they could not bear a knot of sail, but were forced thus to hull [to ride out a storm with no sails set] for divers days together." And in one of the storms, "John Howland, coming upon some occasion above the gratings was, with a seele [tipping] of the ship, thrown into the sea." According to Bradford, "it pleased God that he caught hold of the topsail halyards [long ropes]," which had worked loose in the storm and happened to be trailing in the water. Sailors were then able to pull him back aboard.

During the rough weather, conditions aboard *Mayflower* became increasingly wet and miserable. The air belowdecks smelled foul. Amid the cramped

Sailors constantly worked to keep a ship seaworthy. The crew stayed busy repairing sails, sealing up decks with caulking, and keeping everything secure on the aging Mayflower.

One passenger, William Butten, and one sailor died during the crossing. Their bodies were wrapped in shrouds and dropped overboard. Travel at sea in the 17th century was considered so difficult and dangerous that shipboard deaths were not unexpected. Many Mayflower passengers sought comfort in worship and prayer.

animal pens and crowded cabins, many passengers fell sick. Yet they felt blessed that only one colonist, William Butten, a servant in the Fuller family, died at sea. A sailor also died on the voyage. Some of the passengers observed that this sailor had been the worst in ridiculing the frightened colonists. They believed his death showed the just hand of God at work.

In fair weather, the passengers were allowed up on deck to get fresh air and exercise. Young Francis Billington was probably among them. But in the long spells of bad weather that plagued the two-month crossing, they must have spent many uncomfortable hours cooped up belowdecks. The religious tensions existing between the colonists may have occasionally troubled them. Still, they entertained themselves as well as they could by playing simple games, reading, singing, and telling stories and riddles. One happy event was the birth of Elizabeth Hopkins's son, appropriately named Oceanus.

As *Mayflower* drew closer to land in early November, Master Jones sent sailors aloft as lookouts. Finally, the mariners spotted the high dunes of

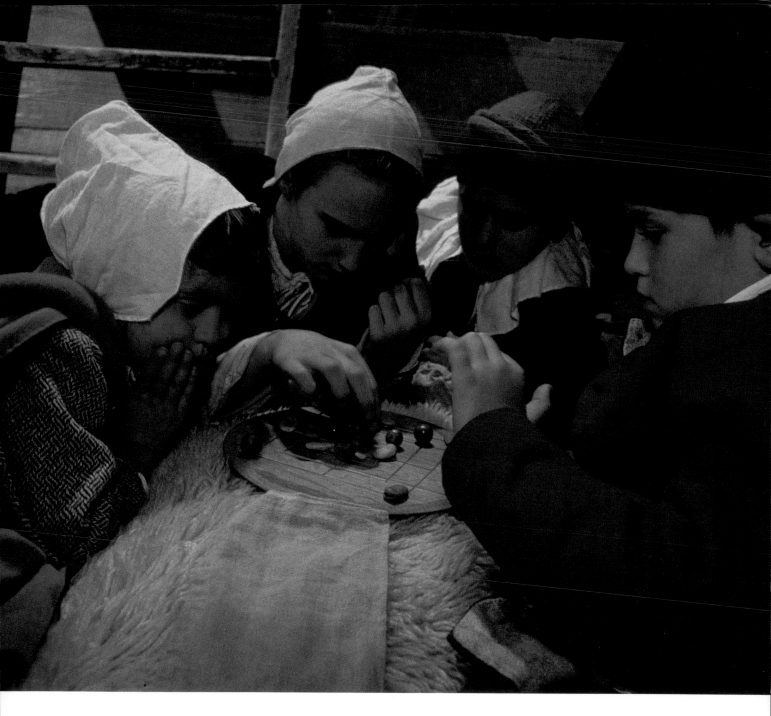

Cape Cod, in the place now known as Massachusetts. They were happy to see land, even though they were about 200 miles northeast of their intended destination. The colonists' contract had granted them land near the Hudson River, so the ship headed south. After trying to sail in dangerously shallow waters in unfavorable winds, Master Jones turned the ship around and brought her to anchor in the harbor at the tip of Cape Cod.

The Mayflower *voyage was long, and there were about 30 children aboard with very little space for play. Nine Men's Morris was a popular children's game that could be played in tight quarters.*

Navigation in the 17th Century

When beyond sight of land, *Mayflower*'s Master Jones relied on his navigational skills and only a few tools to help him reach shore again. He kept the ship on course by using a magnetic compass. To determine latitude—the position north or south of the Equator—he used a cross staff. This tool consisted of a short crosspiece that slid on a long stick marked in degrees. Near noon, the master repeatedly measured the height of the sun by holding the long stick just below his eye and sliding the crosspiece back and forth until it lined up with the sun on the top and the horizon on the bottom. He then noted the angle. After consulting a book of numerical tables and performing some calculations, he could determine the ship's latitude for the day.

He used a chip log to estimate the ship's speed. This small, flat piece of wood attached to a long line on a reel was thrown overboard and floated behind as *Mayflower* sailed ahead. By counting evenly spaced knots in the line as they passed through his hand in a known length of time, the master calculated the speed of the ship in knots, or nautical miles per hour. By multiplying the speed by the number of hours sailed, he could plot the course his ship had covered. He made a series of marks that marched across his chart of the ocean, hoping they would steer him to a safe landfall.

Navigation methods in the 17th century were far from precise. Even skilled navigators could end up off course. With help from two mates who had sailed to America previously, Master Jones landed only one degree north of his goal.

LANDFALL

"...thus arrived in a good harbor and brought safe to land..."

WILLIAM BRADFORD, *OF PLYMOUTH PLANTATION*

It is hard to imagine how it felt to reach land after two months of a dangerous sea voyage. William Bradford wrote: "...[A]fter long beating at sea they fell with that land which is called Cape Cod;...[and] they were not a little joyful....they fell upon their knees, and blessed the God of Heaven, who had brought them over the vast and furious ocean, and delivered them from all the perils and miseries thereof."

Even before going ashore, Francis Billington may have overheard his father muttering to a few other colonists about their contract. Since Cape Cod was north of the specified boundaries, some colonists doubted that the original contract still applied. The leaders of the colony feared that such men might refuse to be governed. To prevent disorder, they restated the terms of the contract in a brief, written agreement that had to be signed before anyone went ashore. This emphasized

When lookouts finally spotted land, both passengers and crew rejoiced. A small workboat called a shallop, which had been stored on Mayflower, *was soon put to use as colonists began exploring Cape Cod for a suitable place to build their new colony.*

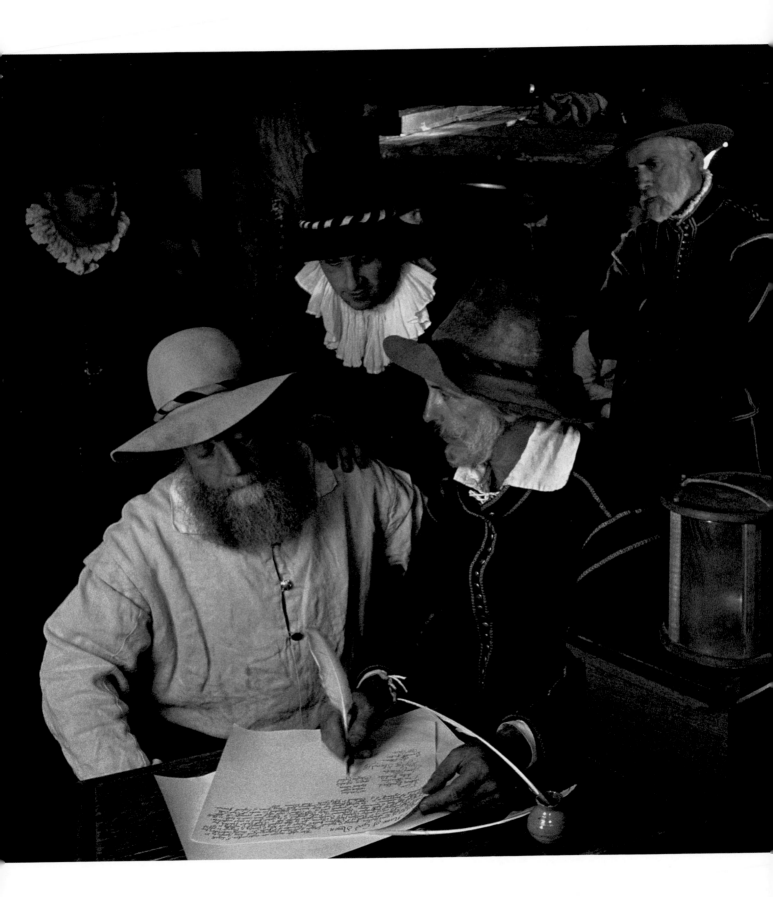

"submission and obedience" to God, the English king, and the company of merchant investors that had granted the colonists permission to settle in English territory. Almost 200 years later, this document became famous as the "Mayflower Compact" when 19th-century historians mistakenly thought they had discovered the beginnings of democracy in it.

Once the ship had anchored, the colonists had much to do. They were happy to be able to get outside, away from their smelly quarters belowdecks. Sailors rowed the women ashore to wash and air clothes. Some of the men set to work repairing the colonists' shallop, the workboat that had been stowed in the passenger quarters. It had been damaged by people sleeping in it during the voyage. Once seaworthy, the shallop would be needed to explore the curving coastline of Cape Cod as the colonists searched for a good place to build their houses before winter arrived.

Some of the men began going on land with armor and muskets. They discovered empty Wampanoag homes and took food, bowls, baskets, and other appealing things from them. They also dug up stores of buried corn, as well as Wampanoag graves. Few of the colonists considered this stealing. Most of them had little or no respect for those they called *Indians* or *savages*.

Before going ashore, colonists had to sign a document drawn up by colony leaders after arrival at Cape Cod. It restated the contract and upheld the leaders' authority.

*Well-armed exploring parties waded
ashore at Cape Cod and surveyed the coast.
Some goods and animals were carried from
Mayflower onto dry land.*

38

Francis Billington got into mischief aboard *Mayflower* in early December. Perhaps he was bored after being confined on the ship for so long. *Mourt's Relation,* a 1622 book about Plymouth Colony, related the incident: "We, through God's mercy, escaped a great danger by the foolishness of a boy, one of…Billington's sons." Francis had shot off his father's gun, "…the fire being within four feet of the bed between the decks…and many people about the fire, and yet, by God's mercy, no harm done."

While the colonists explored Cape Cod, their disrespect for homes and burial grounds provoked some Wampanoag men to shoot arrows at them near Nauset Beach. The Wampanoag were understandably outraged: Europeans from previous ships had brought strange diseases and even kidnapped many of their people. The colonists returned fire with their muskets, but there were no casualties on either side.

After spending a few weeks in Cape Cod, the *Mayflower* passengers decided to look for another place to build their colony. The exploring party boarded the shallop and headed for a harbor across the bay. In a fierce snowstorm, the boat was nearly lost. At nightfall, however, they landed safely on a small island just offshore. The next day, Sunday, was spent in worship and rest. On the following day, the colonists sailed farther into the harbor, hoping to find a good place to settle.

When Mayflower *colonists discovered a supply of dried corn buried at Cape Cod, they dug it up and carried it away. The men brought many of the objects they found back to the ship for everyone to look at. The Native people considered this stealing.*

An Established Nation

Sometimes people say that a person "came over on the *Mayflower*" to indicate that he or she is a member of a very old American family. But the Wampanoag had lived in America long before *Mayflower*'s arrival. For some 12,000 years they had fished the waters, hunted the shores, and planted crops in the sheltered inland areas. Their name means "People of the First Light," but they referred to themselves simply as the People. Their territory was large. It stretched from what is now called Grafton, Massachusetts, to the southeastern corner of Rhode Island and across Cape Cod, Nantucket, and Martha's Vineyard. Their rich culture was organized around family, village, and nation. Their leaders, called sachems, governed by general agreement.

The *Mayflower* colonists were not the first Europeans in Wampanoag territory. Earlier explorers brought trade to the area. They also brought diseases, including plague, which swept through the land from 1616 to 1618. By the time *Mayflower* arrived, sickness had killed so many in Patuxet—the place called Plymouth by the English—that no Wampanoag were left there. To the People, the empty village was a reminder of tragedy and loss. To the colonists, finding tilled fields was a sign of God's favor. They gave little thought to those whose land they were taking over.

Native people had lived in harmony with the land in North America for at least 12,000 years before Europeans arrived.

SETTLEMENT AT "A MOST HOPEFUL PLACE"

On Monday, December 11, 1620, the exploring party from *Mayflower* landed the shallop at the place they would call Plymouth. There is no record that anyone stepped from the boat onto a large rock—later called Plymouth Rock—at this time, but come ashore they did. The colonists found streams with fresh running water, cleared fields, and a good hill for mounting their cannon. To them, it seemed "a most hopeful place" to settle.

The colonists began construction of their new community in late December. A long, cold winter lay ahead. By springtime, half the colonists and half the sailors had perished from exposure, malnutrition, or illness. Despite these hardships, the survivors continued to build their settlement.

In January 1621, young Francis Billington made a discovery of his own in his new home. As told in *Mourt's Relation*, Francis climbed a tree near Plymouth and sighted a large pond, "a great sea as he thought...full of fish and fowl...an excellent help for us in time." Looking around from his treetop perch, Francis would also have seen *Mayflower*, still moored behind him in the bay. The ship would remain there until April 5, 1621, when Master Jones and his crew sailed back to England. Not one of the colonists went along. They were determined to make this land their home.

———————————

Working quickly to raise shelter before winter set in, the settlers built small wooden houses, using reeds to thatch the roofs. During that first winter, many colonists still slept aboard Mayflower *at night.*

BRINGING THE PAST TO LIFE

In April 1621, *Mayflower* sailed back to England. She never returned to North America and was eventually sold for scrap. But since 1957 another ship, *Mayflower II,* has attracted millions of visitors to Plimoth Plantation. Here they learn not only about the reproduction vessel, but also about the significance of the original ship in the context of America's colonial history.

In the summer of 2001, a well-trained crew of staff and volunteers from Plimoth Plantation sailed *Mayflower II* from Plymouth to Boston, Massachusetts. A photography team from National Geographic went along. The purpose of the sail was to create the scenes you have seen in the pages of this book—scenes re-created from the *Mayflower* sail of 1620, nearly 400 years earlier. To curious onlookers aboard the many modern boats that motored alongside the ship as she arrived in Boston, *Mayflower II* must have looked like a visitor from the distant past. And in a way, she is. *Mayflower II* and her staff tell a story about a time in history when enormous changes came to North America.

The meaning of these changes was vastly different for the colonists and the Native people who had already lived for many thousands of years in the so-called New World. For the colonists, the 1620 *Mayflower* was a means of beginning a new life, as well as a link with their home back in Europe. For Native people, the ship was an instrument of change forcing its way into their world—and nearly destroying it. Plimoth Plantation is dedicated to helping modern people reach a better understanding of all facets of our colonial past.

Mayflower II, *shown here at her dock in Plymouth, Massachusetts, sailed from Plymouth to Boston in 2001. Garbed in reproduction colonial-era clothing, interpreters re-created scenes from the first* Mayflower's *voyage.*

A fireboat sprays water to welcome Mayflower II *into Boston Harbor in 2001 (above). A dockside exhibit greets visitors to* Mayflower II *at her berth in Plymouth (near left). Nearby, tourists peer down at Plymouth Rock, where the Pilgrims are traditionally thought to have landed in 1620 (far left). It is uncertain whether the* Mayflower *colonists stepped onto this exact boulder, although they did settle in the area.*

Chronology

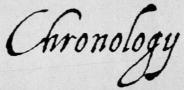

4,000 – 1,000 years ago: Various African, Asian, European, and American cultures began sea travel. Early colonial empires (Egyptian, Greek, Phoenician, Roman, Chinese, Peruvian, Christian, and Islamic) developed maritime trade and warfare.

800 – 1000: Norse mariners colonized Iceland and Greenland and explored coastal North America.

1400s: Portuguese under Prince Henry began circumnavigation of Africa, seeking route to the Orient, establishing colonies, and institutionalizing slave trade.

1492: Christopher Columbus, an Italian navigator sailing for the Spanish, made his first voyage across the Atlantic.

1497: Explorer John Cabot sailed along the east coast of North America, claiming territory for England.

1524: Estevan Gomez, a Portuguese navigator sailing for the Spanish, explored the coast of New England.

1580: Englishman Francis Drake completed a circumnavigation of the globe, looting and claiming land throughout the world for England.

1586: Mathew Baker wrote *Fragments of Ancient Shipwrightery,* the first design for a sail vessel recorded on paper.

1603: Englishman Martin Pring made the first recorded European landing at Patuxet (Plymouth). Other English, French, and Dutch ships began to appear yearly in these waters. The Wampanoag were hospitable; trade was profitable and pleasing to both sides; but cultural differences, misunderstandings, and hostility became evident.

1603: King James of England began pressuring Puritans to conform to the national church. By 1607, some who refused to follow Church of England requirements began leaving for Holland.

1606: Frenchman Samuel de Champlain charted the bay at Patuxet, calling it "Port St. Louis."

1614: Captain John Smith of England named and charted New England and Plymouth. Wampanoag rights to their own homeland were not recognized.

1614: Englishman Thomas Hunt kidnapped more than 20 Wampanoag, including Tisquantum (also called Squanto), for sale as slaves.

1619: Englishman Thomas Dermer returned Tisquantum to his home.

1620: *Mayflower* voyage.

March 1621: Native leaders Samoset, Tisquantum, and Massasoit visited Plymouth and made a treaty with the English.

April 1621: *Mayflower* returned to England.

1625: Plymouth Colony began annual trading with Native people at the Kennebec River, leading to acquisition of colonial patent on lands now in the state of Maine.

1630: John Billington was the first man hanged for murder in Plymouth Colony.

1630s: Thousands of Massachusetts Bay colonists arrived, simultaneously ensuring English support and competition for Plymouth.

1684: Francis Billington died, leaving his wife with some debts and many children and grandchildren. His offspring were loyal to the colony and many became members and even leaders of the colonial church. Billington Sea, a pond in West Plymouth, still bears his family's name.

1692: Plymouth Colony became part of Massachusetts.

1700s: Shipbuilding thrived in many towns along the North River.

1820: Bicentennial celebration of *Mayflower* arrival. Pilgrim Society dedicated Pilgrim Hall Museum, relocating "Plymouth Rock" in front of it. Daniel Webster gave a famous speech praising the Pilgrims as founders of American democracy.

1863: President Lincoln declared the first national Thanksgiving Day, which has been celebrated annually ever since.

1920 – 21: Tercentennial celebration. Renovation of waterfront area around Plymouth Rock.

1947: Plimoth Plantation founded to provide an accurate representation of early Plymouth Colony.

1954: Warwick Charlton organized Project Mayflower and started fund-raising to build *Mayflower II.* Work began on July 4, 1955.

1957: *Mayflower II* sailed from Plymouth, England, to Plymouth, Massachusetts, arriving June 13. Shipmaster Alan Villiers authored two articles for *National Geographic* magazine, bringing international attention to the ship.

1970 – present: Each Thanksgiving Day, many Native people meet at the statue of Massasoit, near Plymouth Rock, to observe a National Day of Mourning.

1991 – present: After nearly three decades of inactivity, *Mayflower II* sailed six times to various ports, including Provincetown and Boston, Massachusetts, and Providence, Rhode Island.

June 2001: *Mayflower II* sailed to Boston. A National Geographic photography team went along to take pictures for this book.

2002: Billington descendants placed a historic marker on a modern office building near the site of the family's first house in the center of what has become downtown Plymouth.

Index

Illustrations are indicated by **boldface.**

Bibliography

1621: A New Look at Thanksgiving, by Catherine O'Neill Grace and Margaret M. Bruchac with Plimoth Plantation (National Geographic Society, 2001)

The Archaeology of Boats and Ships, An Introduction, by Basil Greenhill with John Morrison (Naval Institute Press, 1996)

Early Explorers of Plymouth Harbor, 1525-1619, by Henry F. Howe (Plimoth Plantation and The Pilgrim Society, 1953)

Memory's Nation: The Place of Plymouth Rock, by John Seelye (University of North Carolina Press, 1998)

Men, Ships, and the Sea, by Alan Villiers (National Geographic Society, 1962)

Plymouth Colony: Its History and People 1620-1691, by Eugene Aubry Stratton (Ancestry Publishing, 1986)

The Second Mayflower Adventure, by Warwick Charlton (Little, Brown & Co., 1957)

The Shipwright's Trade, by Westcott Abell (Caravan Book Service, 1962)

The Times of Their Lives: Life, Love, and Death in Plymouth Colony, by James Deetz and Patricia Scott Deetz (W.H. Freeman & Co., 2000)

PRIMARY SOURCE MATERIAL

Mourt's Relation: A Journal of the Pilgrims at Plymouth 1622, edited by Dwight B. Heath (Applewood Books, reprint 1963)

Of Plymouth Plantation 1620-1647, by William Bradford, edited by Samuel Eliot Morison (Alfred A. Knopf, 1952)

A Sea Grammar, by Captain John Smith (London, 1627)

Further resources available by visiting www.plimoth.org

For Sue and the girls — PA
To the memory of Warwick Charlton, and to Marietta Mullen for keeping the flame alive — JCK
For Anne Bagno, *Mayflower* descendant, companion on the journey — COG
To our children, Saskia and Calder — SB & CC

*A*CKNOWLEDGMENTS: Our thanks to the sailing crew of *Mayflower II*, especially Captain Eric Speth, John Brewster, Josh Gedraitis, Paula Marcoux, Doug Ozelius, John Reed, George Ward, and Dave Wheelock, as well as the interpretative staff of Plimoth Plantation for participation in the re-creations that allowed this story to be told. We also thank the staff of Plimoth Plantation, especially Carol City, Linda Coombs, Kathleen Curtin, Jill Hall, Marcia Hix, Liz Lodge, Marietta Mullen, Steve Pekock, Anne Phelan, Maureen Richard, Kathy Roncarati, Carolyn Travers, John Truelson, and Lisa Whalen. We are also grateful to Kendel and Mikel Carr, Charlie Mitchell and the crew of the *Jaguar,* Andy Costa and the crew of the *Andy-Lynn,* and Eric Swanson of the Cedar Hill Retreat Center.

*I*LLUSTRATIONS CREDITS: Cover, Bert Lane/Plimoth Plantation; 2-3, 8, Bert Lane/Plimoth Plantation; 12, Courtesy Thomas Gilcrease Institute of American History and Art; 45 (upper), Bert Lane/Plimoth Plantation.

First paperback printing 2007 ISBN: 0-7922-6276-X\978-0-7922-6276-3
Text copyright © 2003 Plimoth Plantation
Photographs copyright © 2003 Sisse Brimberg and Cotton Coulson
Published by the National Geographic Society. All rights reserved. Reproduction of the whole or any part of the contents without written permission from the publisher is strictly prohibited.

Style design by Suez Kehl Corrado. The text of the book is set in Garamond. The display text is Aquiline and Chanson d'Amour.

The world's largest nonprofit scientific and educational organization, the National Geographic Society was founded in 1888 "for the increase and diffusion of geographic knowledge." Since then it has supported scientific exploration and spread information to its more than eight million members worldwide.

The National Geographic Society educates and inspires millions every day through magazines, books, television programs, videos, maps and atlases, research grants, the National Geographic Bee, teacher workshops, and innovative classroom materials.

The Society is supported through membership dues, charitable gifts, and income from the sale of its educational products.

Members receive NATIONAL GEOGRAPHIC magazine—the Society's official journal—discounts on Society products, and other benefits.

For more information about the National Geographic Society, its educational programs, and publications, or ways to support its work, please call 1-800-NGS-LINE (647-5463), or write to the following address:

National Geographic Society
1145 17th Street, N.W.
Washington, D.C. 20036-4688
U.S.A.

Visit the Society's Web site: www.nationalgeographic.com
For information about special discounts for bulk purchases, please contact National Geographic Books
Special Sales: ngspecsales@ngs.org

Printed in Mexico

Published by the National Geographic Society

John M. Fahey, Jr.   *President and Chief Executive Officer*
Gilbert M. Grosvenor   *Chairman of the Board*
Nina D. Hoffman   *Executive Vice President*
        President of Books and Education Publishing

Staff for this Book

Ericka Markman   *Senior Vice President, President of Children's Books and Education Publishing Group*
Nancy Laties Feresten   *Vice President, Editor-in-Chief, Children's Books*
Bea Jackson   *Art Director, Children's Books*
Jennifer Emmett   *Project Editor*
Alexandra Littlehales   *Designer*
Cotton Coulson and
Elizabeth LaGrua   *Illustrations Editors*
Janet Dustin   *Illustrations Coordinator*
Marfé Ferguson Delano   *Editor*
Jo H. Tunstall   *Assistant Editor*
Carl Mehler   *Director of Maps*
XNR Productions   *Map Research and Production*
Connie D. Binder   *Indexer*
R. Gary Colbert   *Production Director*
Lewis R. Bassford   *Production Manager*
Vincent P. Ryan   *Manufacturing Manager*

The design shown on page one and used throughout as a decorative device is a mayflower carved and painted on the stern of the *Mayflower II.*

Library of Congress Cataloging-in-Publication Data
Plimoth Plantation.
  Mayflower 1620: a new look at a pilgrim voyage / by Plimoth Plantation with Peter Arenstam, John Kemp, and Catherine O'Neill Grace; photographs by Sisse Brimberg and Cotton Coulson.
  p. cm.
  Includes index.
  ISBN: 0-7922-6142-9
  1. Mayflower (Ship)--Juvenile literature. 2. Pilgrims (New Plymouth Colony)--Juvenile literature. 3. Massachusetts--History--New Plymouth, 1620-1691--Juvenile Literature. 5. Plimoth Plantation, Inc.-- Juvenile literature. [1. Mayflower (Ship) 2. Pilgrims (New Plymouth Colony) 3. Masssachusetts-- History--New Plymouth, 1620-1691. 4. Mayflower II (Ship) 5. Plimoth Plantation, Inc.] I. Arenstam, Peter. II. Kemp, John. III. Grace, Catherine O'Neill, 1950- IV. Brimberg, Sisse, ill. V. Coulson, Cotton, ill. VI. Plimoth Plantation, Inc. VII. Title.
  F68.A69 2003
    974.4'8202--dc21
                                    2002155784